Emotionally Unavailable Father

Does he love you? And does it matter?

By

Alyson Jodene

Emotionally Unavailable Father: Does he love you? And does it matter?

Copyright © 2017

All rights reserved. This book or any portion thereof may not be reproduced or used in any manner whatsoever without the express written permission of the publisher except for the use of brief quotations in a book review.

ISBN: 9781520259833

Warning and Disclaimer

Every effort has been made to make this book as accurate as possible. However, no warranty or fitness is implied. The information provided is on an "as-is" basis. The author and the publisher shall have no liability or responsibility to any person or entity with respect to any loss or damages that arise from the information in this book.

Publisher Contact

Skinny Bottle Publishing

books@skinnybottle.com

- Bye-Bye Emotionless Father, Hello Beautiful Me 1
- The Immediate 5
  - Only an A? 5
  - We Deserve Unconditional Love 6
  - King of the Castle, King of None 7
- Dry Wells 9
  - There's Wisdom in That Saying 9
  - Take Your Time 9
- Throwing the Ideal 11
  - Grab the Garlic and Holy Water 11
  - Bye-Bye Mr. Perfect 12
- Drawing the Line 13
  - Who's The Most Important Person in Your Life? 15
- His Early Eulogy 17
  - Humor Me 17
  - From Anger to Acceptance 19
  - Uncharted Imaginary Waters 19
  - Nobody Is Alone, Not Even You 20
- Conclusion 21

Bye-Bye Emotionless Father, Hello Beautiful Me

Like a bird that just flew into the window of a strange house — this is what it feels like growing up in a household where Dad was anything but present.

You look around the house and everything seems foreign. Without love, it feels like you are on somebody else's turf. Like you are just a visitor eventually your time will come to leave.

At least that's what it felt like for me. I felt like I was continually a broken version of whatever I was supposed to be. I couldn't figure out if it was my looks, or my school grades, or maybe because I didn't play sports like my brothers. I looked for an answer everywhere to try and explain why Dad just didn't do anything with me.

At first I thought it was just that he was too busy. I would be proud that Dad would go to work all day. And that at night, when he was home, he wanted to just relax in front of the TV. I felt like he earned that. I would even bring him a drink out of the fridge, served on a tray even though we never really used the TV trays. During those times he wouldn't even bother to utter a single thank you. I was okay with it at first, until I started to learn that he just didn't care about me, at least not like he did my brothers. For a little child, that sort of stuff was hard for me to understand. Only after an adolescence, young adulthood, and even into my mid-30's did I start to grasp that my father was completely emotionally unavailable.

It didn't matter how he treated my brothers. The only thing that I needed to be concerned with was that he was emotionally unavailable to me. That's when I learned how to draw the line. I had to set barriers if I was going to prevent myself from continuing to be the doormat that let my family continually walk over me. It wasn't just my father, it was the whole family dynamics, except my sister, that led me to realize it all centered around my dad's completely vapid emotional wasteland.

I'm writing this now to you, regardless of whether you are a man or a woman, to tell you that you no longer need to let somebody that is emotionally unavailable continue to control your own emotional wellbeing. There is a way. It wasn't easy for me, but I certainly poured many hours, and a lot of money out to counselors, as I tried to make my way through the source of why I was having so many personal problems. It wasn't just my self-esteem that was blown, I couldn't even make a decent relationship last for any significant amount of time.

Every time I met a guy I threw myself on him. I would do anything I could to try and please him. It didn't matter how degrading he made me feel. So long as I could catch a glimpse of the attention I had longed for as a child, I would feel like I had made it to the oasis after a long trek through the desert. It would be sweet long enough for me to realize it was all a mirage. There is nothing that is healthy about those relationships that I put myself through for so many years. I am writing this to you because I hope that you can have a head start on realizing the things that took me 37 years to figure out. That's a long time to carry around that pain.

I am happy to say that I have never been filled with so much light and levity as I am now. My days are filled with joy, abundance, and contentment. Sure, there are times that I start to begin to wallow in my druthers. But that's exactly when I remember that I have to let go of the past and put one foot in front of the other and move forward for there is no other direction to go. The following is my guidance. I hope that you too will begin to feel free. My best wishes to you: stay strong, and please, please, don't let somebody else's pain become your own. Emotions are beautiful. Live and breathe yours. Don't deny them.

The Immediate

Only an A?

One of the hardest things for me growing up was not knowing what to do when I was confronted by a dad that just didn't care. I would come home from school eager to show him my report card only to find that even my A's weren't good enough. He would demand why they weren't all A+ marks. It would have been nice to have some support that I was doing well. Yes, it sounds silly that I am harping about something that happened nearly three decades ago. But I'm sharing it to let you know that you aren't the only one that carries around the emotional scars that we are left with when one of our parents are emotionally abusive.

Surely they don't mean to be abusive. More often than not, when a parent behaves this way, it is almost like they are mirroring the parenting they received themselves. Plus (for most of us) our fathers were part of the generation where men weren't supposed to necessarily tap into their emotions. Their role was to handle the immediate.

They had to put food on the table, a roof over our heads, and provide for us the purely objective things that a person needs to survive. The handbook most of our parents were given, said nothing about a father being there for his children emotionally. This doesn't make it okay for a father to ignore the emotional needs of his child or children.

We Deserve Unconditional Love

When I was younger I would sulk quite often about not getting the response from him that I knew I deserved. When we are born, there is something inside of each of us that knows that we deserve unconditional love. We have nothing but the same to offer the world. Then, over time we get shown the world likes to operate on entirely different principles. When it is one of our parents that is dishing out those principles, it makes for a confusing childhood and leads to a jarring emotional state of well-being, or simply the lack there of.

I'm not a doctor, or licensed psychologist. I feel at this point that my experience trumps anything that I could have ever learned in school. I am however reaching out to you as somebody that has been through this all myself and is a fellow inhabitant of this great wonderful planet. Sometimes the only way you can get over somebody that is passively emotionally distant is to start to learn how to not take it so personally.

I know, I know, this is an achingly horrible thing to hear when you are being emotionally crushed for so long. Especially when, if you are like me, you've heard countless times from your father, or even your whole family, to 'quit being so sensitive'. Don't those words just make your ears ring? They used to mine. Then I learned to embrace my sensitivity, I learned that it wasn't a special trait to me at all. In fact, there was little outlandishly special about me. I was just like everybody else, a throbbing emotional being that expected to be treated with dignity and respect, as I treated others.

Learning how to not take my emotionally distant father so personally was a long arduous road that I hope I can speed up for you. The sooner you get off the road, the sooner you can begin to tap into the wonderful channels of unconditional love and feelings that are openly available to each one of us. But we must work hard to remain unscathed by the thoughtless and cold words of those that are already emotionally stunted and closed-off.

King of the Castle, King of None

There is no quick solution to learning how to deal with a father that is too wrapped up in his own head and problems to step outside of the castle walls he has gated his heart into. That moat is far too wide for you, to try to navigate a safe jump across from the land of reality to his guarded estate. You have to learn to let him be. There is no saving somebody that doesn't want to be saved.

This is a cold hard fact of life. There is no way around this. There are no loopholes, no easy-outs, no what-if's, and most importantly there is nothing that you could have done, can do, or could do that will make the situation any different for him. All you can handle is yourself. That took me years to realize. The more I tried over and over to get him to open up the more I would be shot down by a barrage of ice-tipped arrows straight to my heart. I would cower to my corner and do the figurative wound licking until I was ready for round two, and then sometimes round three, and ten and so on and so forth ad nauseam until I was too old, too tired, and highly disgruntled to continue the pointless battle.

I could have stopped the process earlier and saved myself lots. The only person I could change was me. The same thing applies to you. All you can work on and save is yourself. Yes, it is a horrible thing when it's your parent and they rightfully should be treating you differently. I can almost hear you saying, "Yes, but he did this", and "Yes, but he never", and 'But I need this…"

That's the sort of stuff I used to say. You have all the answers already buried inside you — you know what you need. Unfortunately for you, your journey is very similar to mine, we have to learn to give that deep sense of appreciation and gratitude to ourselves.

What doesn't kill you makes you stronger, right? You, just like I did, will come out the other side, a much stronger, more compassionate person.

Dry Wells

There's Wisdom in That Saying

There's an old saying that goes something like: you don't go to a dry well if you are thirsty. Apply this to your relationship with your father. There comes a point when you realize, that no matter what you do, he is not going to provide the attention you are seeking. The next step is to quit going after it. Yes, it's horribly unfortunate. Parents are supposed to be there for their children, and not just in putting food on the table.

Here is something to remember, even the best parents will at times be emotionally distant from their child's needs. That is just the way it goes. It is impossible, absolutely impossible, for anyone to be able to be there for somebody else one hundred percent of the time. The sooner you realize this and completely accept it, the faster you will be on your way to leading a more fulfilling life that is less focused on what others are giving to you and more focused on your ability to fulfill your life.

Take Your Time

Don't worry. That bridge can be a wide one to cross, and can take a lifetime. The good news is that you can decide for you how long it's going to take you to cross. The time you spend hee-hawing and looking over your past thinking about all the things you never had, is time that could be spent moving forward. You have to quit blaming somebody for not being there for you.

This sounds harsh but I promise you, I mean the best by it. The reason I can say this is because I have been there too. I know exactly what it is like to stand there and wonder what could be different. How many times did I think that I would be more successful or better off in relationships had I been shown a different way?

I would have been better if somebody else didn't mess me up. I would be on my road to leading a more fulfilling life. I stood there on the dark shore of the past continually looking back into it. I couldn't even see that there was a different way at first. After all, how was I supposed to know there was another way to approach life? Guess what? You do know! You are reading this right now, you are resilient, you are strong, and you already refuse to be emotionally tied up any longer! You've got this.

You have to maintain your own. It sucks. It really does. And I hate using those words about as much as I hate using the word hate. Having to compensate for the shortcomings of another person just isn't anyway that a person should have to live. I have chalked this all up to strengthening my ability to discern how I am emotionally affected by another person. Family, or not. Though we all know that family is the most intense. They seem to know all the backdoors right into the secret chambers of the heart. They can cut down the self-esteem like no other. Without even saying a word. How can such big amount of nothing have such an affect? It only has as much as we give it!

Throwing the Ideal

Grab the Garlic and Holy Water

The quickest thing you can do right now to help yourself is to grab your notion of what an ideal father is like and throw it out the window. It doesn't do you any good to harbor feelings and hopes that he is suddenly going to turn the love light on and be there for you. I'm sure you have already done everything you could to get him to open up, only to be met by his stoic reserve, or even worse his bitter and cutting indifference.

There is something to be said about trying to keep your relationship with him in the general faith that people can change. For now, though, put that thought of him changing so far on the backburner that you don't even realize that it is there. Let's face it, if he does change, it's going to be a mixture of miracle and his own undoing. Meanwhile, you have to figure out a way that you can still relate to your father.

Perhaps there are many sides of him that you have not been able to admire fully because you are too concerned with not getting the emotional response out of him that you wish you had. Chances are that he has more than a couple things that interest him. They might not be anywhere close to your interests but let's face it, nobody is going to be here forever. All you can do about today is to try your best to be loving. All you can do is set an example for how you want to be treated. But remember it's about respect, and not about him being like the imaginary father you want.

Bye-Bye Mr. Perfect

You only get one father. Perhaps two, depending on your family dynamics, but your father is just a man. He isn't some superhero that knows how to come to the rescue for every little emergency. Some dads are better at rescuing kittens out of the tree, some dads are better at sitting on the sideline and making fun of the kitten for getting up into the tree. Once you realize that, then you can stop trying to get him to open up about things. No matter how much you think that your Dad needs to share his feelings with you, you have to let go of it.

There is nothing pleasant about this. Don't get me wrong, it is no easy feat. But once you throw away the idea of who you think he should be you can start to see him for who he is. There's a slight chance that you will see him as the very hurt, insecure man that he is. Don't call him out on it. Treating him the way he treats you will only perpetuate the vicious cycle that he is most likely carrying on from his parents and their parents and so on.

It's your responsibility to break the cycle by not playing into that same drama of cold distance, and simply let that notion of having the perfect father fall to the ground. He doesn't exist. Not for you, and beyond a doubt, for anybody else. The perfect father is a myth as make believe as Santa Claus or the Fairy Godmother. Your dad is human just like the rest of us. His life has probably made him respond the way he does. Just keep telling yourself that he just doesn't know any better.

Once you can start seeing him as a wounded soul, you can keep the lights of your love on without dimming them. It's your turn to be the light you were born to be. Explode brightly.

Drawing the Line

Sometimes things are just too extreme. You've been told by others, or even through your own research, on how to handle an emotionally distant father. The advice is clear — you have to do your best to draw the line. But how do you draw the line with somebody that you are supposed to be there for? And what if you are still living at home? There are a couple tricks that I've learned over the years when it comes to drawing the line and I'm more than happy to share them with you:

- You're going to have to draw the line a lot. Like several times a day, sometimes even several times a minute. As you start to set the boundaries between what you will allow for yourself and what you will not, your heart will cave, and your insecurities will waver. Sooner or later you will find that you have let the person (your dad in this case) cross over the line from being somebody that you kept on a short leash to somebody that once again has full-control over how you are feeling. You have to remember that learning to draw the line is a process that you will revisit several times in your life. I am still, to this day, redrawing that line every time I start to think the edge of it is getting dull. Keep that line sharp, and don't beat yourself up for having to redefine your boundaries. You have a whole life to live that you should be out there living. Emotionless Daddy is bound to sneak across the emotional threshold from time to time.

- Don't bother telling him you drew a line. There's no reason to further confide in somebody, that isn't even returning an emotional response, that they have gone too far and that you now need room to breathe from their emotionally stagnant breath. What would the point be? Just to have them ignore you? Treat you like dirt some more? There's no reason that you need to subject yourself to that harsh treatment any longer. Just know where you draw the line and make sure that you stay on your side of it. Drawing the line means that you no longer need to be responsible for jumping through every blazing ring of fire your dad sets up for you.

- Say No and mean it. Sometimes you don't even have to say no. Just don't say yes. Don't continue to allow yourself to be the household emotional doormat. You probably don't know yet what sweet bliss is waiting for you right on the other side of an affirmative and stern demand for the respect you deserve. Just remember that he isn't going to be prepared, or even know how to give you the respect that you want from him. You are going to have to either give him some lampposts to light his way, or kindly let him discover his own way out of those dark woods he likes to wallow in. What's important is that you no longer beat yourself up for his emotional distance, and that you don't hold it against him that he isn't who you wished he'd be. Let bygones be bygones.

- If he is being emotionally distant and treating you like you are his property, you need to draw a quick hard line in that sand. It's understandable during your adolescent years when he might be trying to 'look out for your own good'. This is his own way of saying that he cares. But telling you what to do with your free time as an adult is unacceptable. Perhaps he is having a hard time dealing with the fact that he no longer holds you under his control. He's going to grab at whatever straw he can get just to be able to maintain a splinter of that lost control. You don't have to make a big fiery explosion about him never being there for you. Why waste your fire? Keep yourself in check and rise above the situation. Remember you are the stronger one.

Setting boundaries is difficult when you want your father's attention. It's true that sometimes we take on the negative attention just because it's attention, and let's face it, that's all we have come to expect from somebody that just doesn't know how to treat their own child properly.

Who's The Most Important Person in Your Life?

The trick is to knowing where you house your own sense of self-worth. You have to hold closely on to your own feelings of empowerment. You are the most important person in your own life. I am my own, he is his own, and that's the way it has to be before anybody can even begin to contribute emotionally or rationally to this game of life that we are all in.

When you spend time with him, assuming you haven't kicked him out of your life, you have to carry the mindset that you don't even need armor. You don't need armor because you are high above his negativity. You have to place yourself on such high frequency that you don't even resonate with the very nature of his distance. If you start to feel that you are getting wrapped up in his problems, know when it's time to quit. It's okay to look at him and say, "That's not my problem."

His Early Eulogy

Humor Me

Okay this chapter is harsh. But it's just the way life is, and it isn't all that morbid and dreary. Okay it is. You and I aren't fooling anybody. We know what it's like to harbor those thoughts that perhaps things would be better if we had a different parent, or heck even if we were raised by wolves. Wolves would probably have more emotional nurturing and sense of humanity than Dad ever showed. So let's take this approach seriously. Let's write a eulogy for good 'ole Pa. Yep. Let's pretend he's dead.

- Imagine that you are standing there at his funeral preparing to give a eulogy in his honor. What are you wearing? Are you wearing your best clothes? Are you still in your PJ's? How many people do you see in the room? Perhaps the room is empty, maybe there are only a few people present. When I did it, the room was packed with everybody in the town. There wasn't a soul that wasn't there. I was wearing a pair of black sunglasses, the kind you wear when you go running. I held my self-respect and dignity high. Go ahead, imagine what his funeral is like for you.

- Now it's your time to talk. What are you going to say? Are you going to stand there and tell everyone what a horrible man he was? Go ahead if that's what you need to do. Now is your time to bury those words with him. You can't let a single thing go unheard in your vision. Do you really want to tell the people in the room the truth about what kind of man he was? If not, why? What part of him are you still trying to protect? There he is after all, lying in the coffin beside you dead.

- Do you have nice things to say? Really true and honest, nice things? Try and think of at least five things the man did for you that made a big difference in your life. Even if it was as simple as making sure that you went to school for 8 hours while he stayed home and drank. The monster still did something good for you. Try and find it now. Try hard if you must. But find it. Tell the crowd about it.

- Tell them how you wished he would have been better. Write it out in your eulogy. You have been writing this out haven't you? Really truly write it out. Don't worry, you can always get rid of it when you are done. Shred it up if you must or toss it in a nice bonfire if you can have one where you live.

- Now, in your imaginary funeral, turn to your father, and thank him for making you the strong person that you are. Tell him that you know he was just a man. That even though you wanted him to be a superhero, and that he meant the world to you, that you now realize he was only doing the best he knew how to do, no matter how unsatisfactory it was.

- When you finish finding the courage to thank him, you can now let him go. Say your goodbye and let the funeral continue. In my vision I went so far as riding in a limousine out to a lush gardened cemetery where they were going to put my poor father in a cheap pine box out in this drab location. I pulled out my checkbook and wrote a check right then and there to get him in the best coffin and the best location possible with all of the works. On his imaginary tombstone I put:

18

"You weren't the best man. But you died a forgiven man. May Heaven find you."

Now of course I know this is not how things work out in reality. There is no way to magically whip out a checkbook and stop the proceedings of the funeral right then and there. Perhaps there is, but either way I don't really have that sort of checkbook. But the process helped me a lot. I thought it was a weird suggestion when my counselor told me about it but hey, it worked magic on me. The best thing about it was that from that day moving forward, I could look at my father a little more simply, for he was nothing but a simple man.

From Anger to Acceptance

The wildest thing for me when I did the funeral/eulogy meditation was that I began to love my father more than I did before I started it. When I began the eulogy I was angry, hurt, and riddled with bitterness. Viewing him as a transient being that was simply living his life path out, helped me see him as a cohabitant of this world rather than the defining lead character of my emotional stability. Somehow we had both managed to meet at the crossroads of being family members. My happiness was up to me.

Uncharted Imaginary Waters

When you start walking through your own imaginary eulogy, don't be surprised if you have all sorts of emotions surface that you weren't aware of. It made me think about things a lot differently and honestly I was all sorts of a tear-fest by the time I was imagining him going into the ground.

Obviously we don't do this exercise because we really want our father to die, this is more about the process of seeing them in a transformative light so that you can realize that they will one day slip away.

When it's you standing there at the podium, with eulogy scripted out in hand, and nobody is there to hold your hand, where is your strength going to come from? It has to come from within. You have that powerful and magical fire burning in you. Learn to listen to it, get to know yourself better than anybody else, and hold your head high.

Nobody Is Alone, Not Even You

Not a single one of us is alone in the world, no matter how lonely and terrifying things may seem right now. This too shall pass. You already have all the tools you need inside of you, ready to be used for the right reasons. Next time you are starting to feel the pull that somebody is not appreciating your worth, learn to walk away.

Many of us have had to deal with the pains of having an emotionally distant parent. Just remember there is a difference between distant and abusive. If he is abusive then you should seek professional assistance. Don't hesitate to open your mouth and tell authorities, no matter how much you have been threatened to be silent. Stand up, speak up, and be present in your own life. You have all the power within you already. Listen to your Self, tell yourself you are worth it.

You know what? You are!

Conclusion

Through the process of letting go of my emotional island of a father, I learned to quit seeking approval from anybody but myself. I started to realize that my life was all about my own successes, no matter how big or small they were. I am the one that has to deal with myself when I lie my head down at night. That is me alone in my head. I had rented out room in my mind for him for too long, letting him control my thoughts, my feelings, and ultimately the quality of my every single breath. Life was too suffocating when I was trying to constantly appeal to his every whim, which was next to impossible to understand.

Now that I stand on the other side of the line, the one that I drew between him and me years ago, I can see him for what he is. I can tell you that it is not a pretty sight. It is sad, and he has lost a lot of the sense of being noble like I once thought him to be. It's no easy way of life, having to let go of a parent the way I have, and the way you too might have to do.

I still see people wandering around, especially during the holiday seasons or when it's nice out at the park, and I think to myself why couldn't that be me and my dad? Then, when I start to get that sinking feeling in my stomach, I remind myself that I'm doing nothing but beating myself up. Whenever I let those feelings take control of me I am doing nothing but comparing myself to others, although I have no idea what their life is like behind closed doors.

I hope that you can begin to see now that you are the only one that is responsible for how you feel. You are also the only one that can control how others make you feel. The way you have been treated may be wrong, but I'm not here to tell you to 'toughen up' like I was once told. I am here to remind you there is nothing you can do to make somebody suddenly open up. You can't take on charity cases either, even if it is your father. You have to put your own emotional well-being and happiness at the top of your totem pole. If you aren't the first one up there, then who are you living your life for?

No other person on the face of the planet can take as good of care of you, as you can yourself. The more you begin to fulfill your own sense of security the more you will learn to trust others. Trust has always been something that I struggled with through my years of growing up. Why should I let somebody else in just so they could take advantage of me like my father had? Eventually though, when I learned how to rely on myself, I could extend more trust to others because I wasn't putting so much of my own emotional stability into somebody else's hands.

I am happy to say that I hope I am never that trusting to give somebody all of my emotional security. I no longer believe that giving somebody complete control over my emotions is a sign of being in love. My idea of love has grown over the years to be more inclusive and unconditional. I have also learned to not accept anything but the same from those that I let into my personal life. That includes friends, dates, and even my professional life. I do not let negativity anywhere near me. When it comes close I remember that it is me that is the one that has to draw the line, or else the other person will just keep walking all over me.

I pass this on to you, so you may become victorious with your emotional health. Just because somebody is emotionally distant, especially a dad, doesn't mean that you aren't worthy or that you aren't beautiful. You are all of those things and then some! Just keep reminding yourself until you fully believe it too. Eventually it catches on, and once it does watch out world, here you come!

Win a free

kindle
OASIS

Let us know what you thought of this book to enter the sweepstake at:

http://booksfor.review/unavailablefather

Made in the USA
Monee, IL
02 December 2022